The *Speedy* Revision Guide

Key Stage 3
Tier 3–5

Speedy Revision

Introduction

This revision guide is aimed at Tier 3–5 of the KS3 National Tests for Mathematics. It's the perfect size to keep with you at all times during the crucial weeks before the tests.

There is *speedy* coverage of each topic in the four main strands:
- Number
- Algebra
- Shape, space & measures
- Handling data

Everything you need to know about a topic is given on one or two pages, in the same format:
- **Essential facts**
  Everything you need to know, complete with examples.
- **Q & A**
  Easy-to-follow worked examples with clearly explained methods.
- **Check-up TESTs**
  To make sure everything has sunk in. (If you can do all the tests, you are heading in the right direction!)

On pages 55–58 there is a *speedy* revision test to check that you have remembered all the basic facts. (If you're short of time, try the revision test first, then revise those topics you got wrong; that truly is *speedy* revision!)

Good luck in your tests!

Contents

Place value (1)

● Big numbers

875 is 'eight hundred and seventy-five' in words.

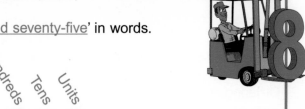

Hundreds Tens Units

8 7 5

800   +   70   +   5   = 875

eight hundred   and   seventy   five

Split bigger numbers into groups of three, starting from the right:

Hundreds Tens Units
of Thousands   Hundreds Tens Units

3 2   5 4 9

Then read
from the left:

32 549 is 'thirty-two THOUSAND, five hundred and forty-nine'.

● Decimals

❶ Write the number to the left of the decimal point as before.

❷ Then write 'point'.

❸ Then list the digits to the right of the decimal point.

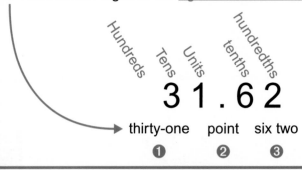

Hundreds Tens Units   tenths hundredths

3 1 . 6 2

thirty-one   point   six two

❶   ❷   ❸

Place value (2)

● Multiplying by 10, 100 or 1000

To multiply by:

Th	H	T	U
		3	7

10 move the digits <u>1 place left</u> $37 \times 10 =$ 3 7 0

100 move the digits <u>2 places left</u> $37 \times 100 =$ 3 7 0 0

1000 move the digits <u>3 places left</u> $37 \times 1000 =$ 3 7 0 0 0

● Dividing by 10, 100 or 1000

To divide by:

Th	H	T	U
4	0	0	0

10 move the digits <u>1 place right</u> $4000 \div 10 =$ 4 0 0

100 move the digits <u>2 places right</u> $4000 \div 100 =$ 4 0

1000 move the digits <u>3 places right</u> $4000 \div 1000 =$ 4

● Decimals (×/÷ by 10, 100 or 1000)

The rules are just the same for decimals:

	Hundreds	Tens	Units	.	tenths	hundredths
			1	.	8	
$1.8 \times 10 =$		1	8			
$1.8 \times 100 =$	1	8	0			
		1	4	2		
$142 \div 10 =$		1	4	.	2	
$14.2 \div 10 =$			1	.	4	2

---

1 Write in words: **a** 92   **b** 1603   **c** 15.67

2 Write in figures: **a** four hundred and ten   **b** two point eight

3 **a** 39×10 **b** 8×1000 **c** 7.1×10 **d** 1.5×100
  e $420 \div 10$ **f** $6400 \div 100$ **g** $16.3 \div 10$ **h** $149 \div 100$

TEST

Mental strategies for + and –

● Partitioning

➤ Q & A

a 145 + 213   **b** 683 – 274

Answer

a Re-write the sum with the larger number first:

213 + 145

Add 145 a bit at a time:

213 + 100 + 40 + 5 = <u>358</u>

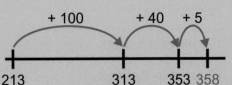

b Subtract 274 a bit at a time:

683 – 200 – 70 – 4 = <u>409</u>

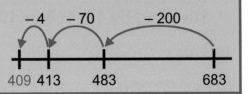

● Compensation

I could do with some compensation.

➤ Q & A

a 357 + 52   **b** 718 – 496

Answer

a Round 52 down to 50, then compensate:

357 + 52

= 357 + 50 + 2

= 407 + 2

= <u>409</u>

b Round 496 up to 500, then compensate:

718 – 496

= 718 – 500 + 4

= 218 + 4

= <u>222</u>

● Other useful tricks

Look out for <u>near doubles</u>: 150 + 160 = double 150 + 10 = 310

Find <u>pairs totalling 10</u>: 9 + 7 + 1 + 3 = <u>9 + 1</u> + <u>7 + 3</u> = 10 + 10 = 20

---

1 Use partitioning to answer these:

    a 418 + 67   **b** 112 + 375   **c** 893 – 46   **d** 510 – 146

2 Use compensation to answer these:

    a 58 + 73   **b** 346 + 207   **c** 489 – 64   **d** 782 – 517

TEST

Speedy Revision

Written methods for + and –

● Whole numbers

➤ Q & A

a 139 + 57

b 723 – 382

Answer

a

```
  1 3 9
+   5 7
  1 9 6
  1
```

9 + 7 = 16
Carry the '1' to
the tens column.

> ➤ **Method**
> ❶ Line up the units.
> ❷ Add/subtract the units first.
> ❸ Then tens, then hundreds.

Answer

b

```
  ⁶7̷¹2̷ 3
-  3 8 2
   3 4 1
```

2 is less than 8
so 'borrow' a ten.
12 – 8 = 4

● Decimals

➤ Q & A

a 4.72 + 3.51

b 57.3 – 41.2

Answer

a

```
  4 . 7 2
+ 3 . 5 1
  8 . 2 3
  1
```

7 + 5 = 12
Carry the '1' to the
units column.

> ➤ **Method**
> ❶ Line up the units.
> ❷ Add/subtract a column at a time, starting on the <u>right</u>.

Answer

b

```
  5 7 . 3
- 4 1 . 2
  1 6 . 1
```

---

1 Use a written method to calculate:
   a 251 + 143   **b** 591 + 286   **c** 579 – 141   **d** 703 – 92
2 Use a written method to calculate:
   a 5.16 + 2.73   **b** 1.49 + 2.35   **c** 2.39 – 2.14   **d** 17.98 – 5.71

TEST

Ordering numbers

● Symbols you should know

= means 'is equal to'

< means 'is less than', e.g. 3 < 4

> means 'is greater than', e.g. 4 > 3

≤ means 'is less than or equal to'

≥ means 'is greater than or equal to'

> ### Example
> If 13 016 ≤ ☐ ≤ 13 599 then 13 016 could go in the box, or 13 599, or any number in between.

● In the middle

Use a number line to find the number halfway between 2 numbers.

The number halfway between 18 940 and 18 950 is 18 945.

18 940   18 945   18 950

● Ordering whole numbers

> ### Q & A

Put these in order, smallest first:
999, 2012, 1998, 152, 56, 4162

Answer

2-digits   3-digits   4-digits

56, 999, 152, 2012, 1998, 4162

56, 152, 999, 1998, 2012, 4162

> ### Method
> ❶ Write any 1-digit numbers first, then 2-digit numbers, then 3-digit numbers, ...
> ❷ Put each group in order.

● Ordering decimals

To find out whether 4.16 is greater than 4.128, write them underneath each other, with the decimal points lined up.

4 . 1 6

4 . 1 2 8

same same

6 > 2

Compare the digits in the first column <u>from the left</u> where the digits are <u>not the same</u>.

6 > 2 so 4.1<u>6</u> > 4.1<u>2</u>8

---

1   Find the number halfway between 34 000 and 34 600.

2   Put in order, smallest first: 516, 209, 33, 1460, 888

3   Which is greater, 23.19 or 23.25?

TEST

Rounding & estimating (1)

● Rounding to the nearest 10

To round 8632 to the nearest 10 you need to decide whether it is closer to 8630 or 8640.

Sketch a number line to find out.

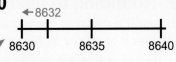

8632 is closer to 8630.
8632 is 8630 to the nearest 10.

For numbers that are exactly halfway, always round up.

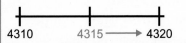

4315 is exactly halfway between 4310 and 4320.
So 4315 is 4320 to the nearest 10.

● Rounding to the nearest 100 or 1000

➤ Q & A

Round **a** 8350 to the nearest 100 **b** 6790 to the nearest 1000.

Answer

a 8350 is between 8300 and 8400.
It is exactly halfway.
So 8350 is 8400 to the nearest 100.

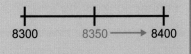

b 6790 is between 6000 and 7000.
It is closest to 7000.
So 6790 is 7000 to the nearest 1000.

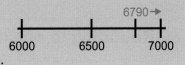

● Estimating calculations

Always check answers to calculations by estimating.

For example, 519 + 34 is roughly 520 + 30 = 550.

Now use 'compensation' (page 6) to find the exact answer. Go on!

You should get 553, which is close to 550, so you can be confident you haven't made a ridiculous mistake.

Always make an estimate

---

1 Round to the nearest 10: **a** 79 **b** 435 **c** 1067
2 Round to the nearest 1000: **a** 1051 **b** 500 **c** 16 800
3 Do you think 489 + 204 = 936 is correct? Explain.

TEST

Rounding & estimating (2)

● Rounding to the nearest whole number

To round a decimal to the nearest whole number, you must decide whether it is closer to the whole number below or the one above.

As before, if it is <u>exactly halfway</u> you <u>round up</u>.

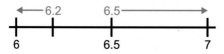

6.2 is closer to 6 than 7. So 6.2 is <u>6 to the nearest whole number</u>.
6.5 is exactly halfway, so it is <u>7 to the nearest whole number</u>.

● Rounding without a number line

You don't have to draw a number line to see whether to round a number up or down.

When rounding to the nearest whole number, look at the <u>tenths digit</u>.

If it is <u>less than 5</u> you <u>round down</u>.
If it is <u>5 or more</u> you <u>round up</u>.

> **➤ Examples**
> In 6.<u>2</u> the tenths digit is 2.
> 2 < 5 so round down to 6.
> In 6.<u>5</u> the tenths digit is 5.
> 5 ⩾ 5 so round up to 7.

● Rounding to one decimal place (1 d.p.)

Rounding to 1 d.p. means rounding to the <u>nearest tenth</u>.

To see whether to round to the tenth above or below, look at the next place – the hundredths digit.

3.2<u>7</u> has 7 in the next place.

7 ⩾ 5 so round up.

3.27 is 3.3 to 1 d.p.

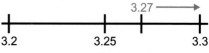

3.27 is more than halfway.

Note: 2.98 is 3.0 to 1 d.p. <u>not</u> 3.
The zero shows it is to 1 d.p. not to the nearest whole number.

1 Round to the nearest whole number:
   a 3.1 **b** 7.6 **c** 2.5 **d** 17.8 **e** 27.3 **f** 3.16 **g** 4.99
2 Round these to 1 d.p. **a** 4.61 **b** 6.45 **c** 1.32 **d** 3.97

Speedy Revision

Negative numbers

● Temperatures on a thermometer

Temperatures on a thermometer can be positive or negative.

Numbers <u>more than 0</u> are <u>positive numbers</u>.
e.g. 5, 10, ...
Numbers <u>less than 0</u> are <u>negative numbers</u>.
e.g. –5, –10, ...

–10°C is <u>less than</u> –5°C, as it is <u>lower down</u> the thermometer.
You can write this as –10 < –5.

Numbers getting bigger: temperatures getting hotter.

Numbers getting smaller: temperatures getting colder.

● Ordering negative numbers

You can order these:
–2, 3, 1, –4, 5
on a number line.

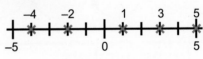

In order, smallest first: –4, –2, 1, 3, 5

● Adding & subtracting negative numbers

Count <u>on</u> when you <u>add</u>.
$$-3 + 5 = 2$$

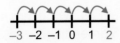

Start at –3 and go on 5.

Count <u>back</u> when you <u>subtract</u>.
$$-1 - 7 = -8$$

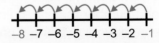

Start at –1 and go back 7.

---

1 Look at the thermometer. Which is smaller, 5 or –10?

2 Put these in order, smallest first: 2, 0, –4, –5, 3

3 Show on a number line: **a** –8 + 3 **b** –2 – 3

TEST

Special numbers

● Even and odd numbers

Even numbers end in 0, 2, 4, 6 or 8 and are exactly divisible by 2.
All other numbers are odd numbers – they end in 1, 3, 5, 7 or 9.

● Square numbers

Square numbers are whole numbers multiplied by themselves.

> ➤ **Example**
> '3 squared' is 3 × 3 = 9.
> '3 squared' is written 3^2.

$1^2 = 1$ $2^2 = 4$ $3^2 = 9$ $4^2 = 16$ $5^2 = 25$

● Triangular numbers

Start at 1 and add 2, then 3, then 4, ...

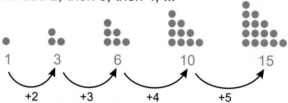

1   3   6   10   15

+2   +3   +4   +5

● Prime numbers

A prime number has exactly two factors (itself and 1).

Note: 1 is not a prime number (it has only one factor – itself).

You should memorise the first few primes: 2, 3, 5, 7, 11, 13, 17, ...
Apart from 2, primes are always odd numbers.
Any odd number that's in a times-table other than its own is not a prime number. e.g. 9 is not prime as it's in the 3 times-table.

---

1 Write down the first ten
   a even   **b** odd   **c** square   **d** triangular numbers.
2 32, 49, 17, 21, 36, 3, 64
   From the list, write down the
   a even   **b** odd   **c** square   **d** triangular   **e** prime numbers.

TEST

Speedy Revision

Multiples & factors

● Multiples

The multiples of a number are the numbers in its times-table.

> ## ➤ Example
> The 3 times-table is:
> $1 \times 3 = 3$, $2 \times 3 = 6$, $3 \times 3 = 9$ ...
> The multiples of 3 are: 3, 6, 9, ...

● Factors

The factors of a number are the numbers that divide into it exactly (including 1 and itself).

You can use these tests to find out the factors of a number:

If it is even, then 2 is a factor. (Even numbers end in 0, 2, 4, 6 or 8.)

If the sum of the digits is a multiple of 3, then 3 is a factor.

If the sum of the digits is a multiple of 9, then 9 is a factor.

If half the number is an even number, then 4 is a factor.

If it ends in 0 or 5, then 5 is a factor.

If it ends in 0, then 10 is a factor.

➤ Q & A

Are 2, 3, 4, 5 and 10 factors of 310?

Answer

310 ends in 0, so 2, 5 and 10 are factors.

$3 + 1 + 0 = 4$ which is not a multiple of 3, so 3 is not a factor.

Half 310 = 155 which is odd, so 4 is not a factor.

● Factor pairs

You can find the factors of a number in pairs:

2 is a factor of 10
and $2 \times 5 = 10$
so 5 is also a factor.

2×5 is a factor pair of 10.

> ## ➤ Example
> The only ways to make 10 are:
> 1×10 and 2×5
> So the only factors are:
> 1, 2, 5 and 10

---

1 List the first five multiples of these: **a** 5 **b** 8 **c** 6 **d** 9
2 Are 2, 3, 4, 5 and 10 factors of 270?
3 List all the factors of these: **a** 8 **b** 32 **c** 40

TEST

Squares & square roots

● Squaring numbers

To square a number, just multiply it by itself.

4^2 is shorthand for '4 squared' or '4 × 4'.

Make sure you know all the square numbers up to 12 × 12:

1, 4, 9, 16, 25, 36, 49, 64, 81, 100, 121, 144

> **Examples**
>
> 1 × 1 = 1
>
> 2 × 2 = 4
>
> 3 × 3 = 9
>
> and so on

> **Q & A**

What is 30^2?

Answer

Say this as 'thirty squared'.

Write what 30^2 means:	$30^2 = 30 \times 30$
Write 30 as 3 × 10:	$= 3 \times 10 \times 3 \times 10$
Put the 10s at the end:	$= 3 \times 3 \times 10 \times 10$ (or $3^2 \times 10^2$)
Multiply the 3s and the 10s:	$= 9 \times 100$
Finish multiplying:	$= \underline{900}$

● Square roots

Finding the square root is the opposite of finding the square.

'What is the square root of 16?' means the same as 'What number squared is 16?'

> **Example**
>
> $\sqrt{16} = 4$
>
> as 4 × 4 = 16

● Powers & roots on your calculator

You should have some buttons like these on your calculator:

To work out 4^2 press **4** $\boxed{x^2}$ **=**. The answer is 16.

To work out $\sqrt{169}$, press $\boxed{\sqrt{}}$ **1 6 9 =** or **1 6 9** $\boxed{\sqrt{}}$. The answer is <u>13</u>. See which works on your calculator.

---

1 Find these squares: **a** 5^2 **b** 11^2 **c** 8^2 **d** 40^2

2 Find these square roots: **a** $\sqrt{36}$ **b** $\sqrt{49}$ **c** $\sqrt{144}$

Check your answers on your calculator.

TEST

 Speedy Revision

Fractions (1)

A fraction shows the number of parts out of the whole.

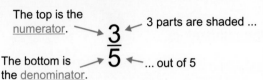

The top is the numerator.

3 parts are shaded ...

$\frac{3}{5}$

... out of 5

The bottom is the denominator.

> ➤ **Example**
>
> $\frac{3}{5}$ is three-fifths.
>
> $\frac{3}{5}$ means 3 out of 5.

● **Equivalent fractions**

Equivalent fractions look the same.

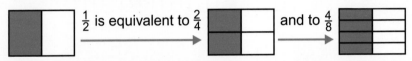

$\frac{1}{2}$ is equivalent to $\frac{2}{4}$ and to $\frac{4}{8}$

You can find equivalent fractions by multiplying or dividing top and bottom (numerator and denominator) by the same number.

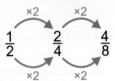

$$\frac{1}{2} \quad \overset{\times 2}{\curvearrowright} \quad \frac{2}{4} \quad \overset{\times 2}{\curvearrowright} \quad \frac{4}{8}$$

$\times 2$ $\times 2$

● **Simplifying fractions**

To simplify a fraction divide top and bottom by the same number. If you can't divide any more you have the simplest form.

➤ **Q & A**

Write $\frac{15}{45}$ in its simplest form.

Answer

Divide by 5: $\frac{15}{45} = \frac{3}{9}$ then divide by 3: $\frac{3}{9} = \frac{1}{3}$

You can't divide any more, so $\frac{1}{3}$ is the simplest form.

---

1 Write down the fraction that is shaded:

2 Write as a fraction in its simplest form:

   a $\frac{4}{6}$ **b** $\frac{12}{16}$ **c** 4p out of 10p (Hint: 10 parts worth 1p each)

TEST

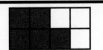

Fractions (2)

● Adding fractions

You can only add fractions if they have the <u>same denominator</u>.

You add them by <u>adding the numerators</u>.

Remember:
The <u>numerator</u> is the <u>top</u>.
The <u>denominator</u> is the <u>bottom</u>.

▶ Q & A

Work out $\frac{2}{9} + \frac{1}{9} + \frac{1}{9}$.

Answer

$\frac{2}{9} + \frac{1}{9} + \frac{1}{9}$

$= \frac{2 + 1 + 1}{9}$

$= \frac{4}{9}$

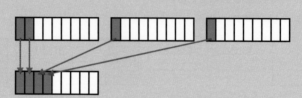

● Subtracting fractions

You can only subtract fractions if they have the <u>same denominator</u>.

You subtract them by <u>subtracting the numerators</u>.

▶ Q & A

Work out $\frac{5}{8} - \frac{3}{8}$. Give your answer in its simplest form.

Answer

$\frac{5}{8} - \frac{3}{8} = \frac{5 - 3}{8}$

$= \frac{2}{8}$

Divide top and bottom by 2

$= \frac{1}{4}$

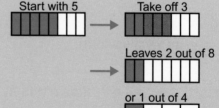

Start with 5   →   Take off 3

Leaves 2 out of 8

or 1 out of 4

---

1 **a** $\frac{1}{7} + \frac{1}{7}$ **b** $\frac{1}{5} + \frac{1}{5} + \frac{1}{5}$ **c** $\frac{2}{9} + \frac{2}{9} + \frac{1}{9}$

2 **a** $\frac{8}{9} - \frac{3}{9}$ **b** $\frac{2}{5} + \frac{1}{5} - \frac{1}{5}$ **c** $\frac{5}{8} + \frac{5}{8} - \frac{3}{8}$

3 Calculate $\frac{7}{10} + \frac{3}{10} - \frac{6}{10}$. Simplify your answer.

TEST

Speedy Revision

Fractions (3)

● Improper & mixed fractions

Improper fractions are 'top heavy', i.e. the numerator is bigger than the denominator.

Mixed numbers are made up of a whole number and a fraction.

➤ Q & A

a Write $2\frac{1}{4}$ as an improper fraction.

b Write $\frac{5}{2}$ as a mixed number.

Answer

a $2\frac{1}{4} = 1 + 1 + \frac{1}{4}$

$\qquad = \frac{4}{4} + \frac{4}{4} + \frac{1}{4}$

$\qquad = \frac{4 + 4 + 1}{4}$

$\qquad = \frac{9}{4}$

b $\frac{5}{2} = \frac{2 + 2 + 1}{2}$

$\qquad = \frac{2}{2} + \frac{2}{2} + \frac{1}{2}$

$\qquad = 1 + 1 + \frac{1}{2}$

$\qquad = 2\frac{1}{2}$

● Ordering fractions

Order fractions by sketching a number line.

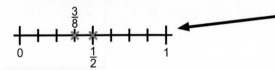

The number line shows that:

$\frac{3}{8} < \frac{1}{2}$

➤ Q & A

Put these in order, smallest first: $2\frac{3}{4}$, $1\frac{1}{2}$, 2, $2\frac{1}{4}$

Answer

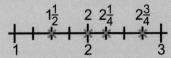

So the correct order is:

$1\frac{1}{2}$, 2, $2\frac{1}{4}$, $2\frac{3}{4}$

---

1 Write $1\frac{2}{3}$ as an improper fraction.

2 Write $\frac{10}{3}$ as a mixed number.

3 Put in order, smallest first: $\frac{7}{8}$ $\frac{1}{2}$ $\frac{3}{4}$

TEST

Fractions, decimals & percentages (1)

● Percentages

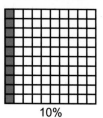

10%

> 'Per cent' means 'out of 100'.

So '10 per cent' means '10 out of 100'.

$$10\% = \frac{10}{100} \text{ or } \frac{1}{10}$$

The % symbol can be used in place of the words 'per cent'.

● Fraction of

To find one-third of something you divide by three.

To find two-thirds, you find a third then multiply by two.

You can find other fractions exactly the same way – find one part then multiply.

> **Example**
> $\frac{1}{3}$ of £60 = £60 ÷ 3 = £20
> ↓ ×2   ↓ ×2
> $\frac{2}{3}$ of £60 = £20 × 2 = £40

● Percentage of

You need to know that:

10% is one-tenth so to find 10% divide by 10

25% is one-quarter so to find 25% divide by 4

> **Examples**
> 10% of £50
> = £50 ÷ 10 = £5
>
> 25% of £12
> = £12 ÷ 4 = £3

➤ Q & A

What is 30% of £500?

Answer

❶ Find 10% first: £500 ÷ 10 = £50

❷ 30% is 3 lots of 10%: 3 × £50 = £150

> **Method**
> ❶ Find 10%.
> ❷ Find however many lots of 10% you need.

---

1 Find: **a** $\frac{1}{5}$ of 120 cm **b** $\frac{3}{5}$ of 120 cm

2 Find 5% of £80. (Hint: 5% is half of 10%)

3 Find 35% of £120. (Hint: 35% is 30% + 5%)

TEST

Fractions, decimals & percentages (2)

● Equivalents you should know

$\frac{1}{2} = 0.5 = 50\%$ $\frac{1}{10} = 0.1 = 10\%$ $\frac{1}{3} = 0.333... = 33\frac{1}{3}\%$

$\frac{1}{4} = 0.25 = 25\%$ $\frac{1}{100} = 0.01 = 1\%$ $\frac{2}{3} = 0.666... = 66\frac{2}{3}\%$

$\frac{3}{4} = 0.75 = 75\%$ $\frac{1}{8} = 0.125 = 12.5\%$

➤ Q & A

Convert $\frac{3}{10}$ to a decimal. $\frac{1}{10} = 0.1$

Answer

$\frac{3}{10} = \frac{1}{10} + \frac{1}{10} + \frac{1}{10} = 0.1 + 0.1 + 0.1 = \underline{0.3}$

● Converting percentages to fractions

Write the percentage as a fraction with denominator 100.

➤ $40\% = \frac{40}{100} = \frac{2}{5}$ Simplify if you can.

● Converting fractions to percentages

Write the fraction as an equivalent fraction with denominator 100.

Then write the numerator with a % sign.

➤ **Example**

$\frac{1}{5} = \frac{20}{100} = 20\%$

● Converting percentages to decimals

This is pretty simple, just divide by 100. Remember to get rid of the % symbol. (See page 5 for the easy way to divide by 100.)

➤ **Example**

$15\% = 15 \div 100 = 0.15$

● Converting decimals to fractions

If there is one decimal place, write it over 10.

If there are two decimal places, write them over 100.

➤ **Example**

$0.8 = \frac{8}{10} = \frac{4}{5}$

$0.12 = \frac{12}{100} = \frac{3}{25}$

Simplify fractions when possible.

---

1 Convert to fractions: **a** 11% **b** 5% **c** 0.6 **d** 0.15
2 Convert $\frac{7}{10}$ to **a** a decimal **b** a percentage.
3 Convert 0.35 to a fraction.

TEST

Mental strategies for × and ÷

● Strategies for multiplying

To multiply by 4, double then double again.

To multiply by 5, multiply by 10 then halve.

To multiply by 9, multiply by 10 then subtract the original number.

To multiply by 11, multiply by 10 then add the original number.

To multiply by 19, multiply by 20 then subtract the original number.

To multiply by 20, multiply by 10 then double.

To multiply by 21, multiply by 20 then add the original number.

To multiply by 25, multiply by 100 then divide by 4.

To multiply by 49, multiply by 50 then subtract the original number.

To multiply by 50, multiply by 100 then halve.

To multiply by 51, multiply by 50 then add the original number.

● Partitioning a multiplication

15 × 7 means '15 lots of 7'.

Because 15 is 10 + 5, you can split '15 lots of 7'
into '10 lots of 7' and '5 lots of 7'.

► Q & A

Calculate 15 × 7.

Answer

$10 \times 7 = 70$

$+ \underline{\ 5 \times 7 = \ 35}$ [to multiply by 5, multiply by 10 then halve]

$15 \times 7 = 105$

● Using times-tables to divide

'Work out 27 ÷ 9' means the same as '9 × ? = 27'.

You know from your times-tables that 9 × 3 = 27, so 27 ÷ 9 = 3.

Do these questions mentally.

1 Calculate: **a** 14 × 4 **b** 23 × 9 **c** 110 × 7 **d** 17 × 12

2 Work out: **a** 56 ÷ 8 **b** 72 ÷ 9 **c** 121 ÷ 11

TEST

Speedy Revision

Written multiplication

● Grid method

➤ Q & A

Use the grid method to work out 29 × 42.

Answer

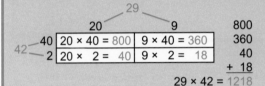

	20	9	
40	20 × 40 = 800	9 × 40 = 360	800
2	20 × 2 = 40	9 × 2 = 18	360
			40
			+ 18

42 {40, 2}

29 × 42 = 1218

➤ Method

❶ Split 29 and 42 into tens and units.

❷ Multiply top number by side number in each box.

❸ Add the four products.

● Column method

If you prefer, you can use the column method for multiplying numbers like 52 × 17.

➤ Example

$$52$$
$$\times \ 17$$
$$52 \times 10 = \quad 520$$
$$52 \times \ 7 = + 364$$
$$52 \times 17 = \quad 884$$

● Multiplying a decimal

If one of the numbers is a decimal, you can still use the grid method or the column method.

➤ Q & A

Work out 7.18 × 9.

Answer

Find 718 × 9 then divide by 100.

Grid method:

7.18 = 7 + 0.1 + 0.08

×	7	0.1	0.08
9	7 × 9 = 63	0.1 × 9 = 0.9	0.08 × 9 = 0.72

63 + 0.9 + 0.72 = 64.62

Column method:

7.18 × 9 = 718 × 9 ÷ 100

$$718$$
$$\times \ 9$$
$$700 \times 9 = 6300$$
$$10 \times 9 = \quad 90$$
$$8 \times 9 = + \ 72$$
$$718 \times 9 = 6462 \xrightarrow{\div 100} 64.62$$

1   Use the grid method: **a** 36 × 23 **b** 121 × 14 **c** 6.42 × 7

2   Check your answers to **Q1** using the column method.

TEST

Written division

● Whole numbers

Keep taking off multiples of the divisor (the number you're dividing by) until you can't subtract any more.

Then add the 'lots' you used.
So if you took off <u>10</u> lots and <u>7</u> lots, the answer is <u>10 + 7 = 17</u>.

> ➤ **Example**
>
> $136 \div 8$
>
> $8\,\overline{)\,136}$
> $\underline{-\ 80} \qquad 10 \times 8$
> $\quad\ 56$
> $\underline{-\ 56} \qquad 7 \times 8$
> $\qquad 0$
>
> Answer = <u>17</u>

● Remainders

Sometimes you will not be able to get to zero, and you will have to give a remainder as part of the answer.

➤ Q & A

Work out $452 \div 6$.

Answer

$6\,\overline{)\,452}$
$\underline{-\ 420} \qquad 70 \times 6$
$\quad\ \ 32$
$\underline{-\ 30} \qquad 5 \times 6$
$\qquad\ 2$

2 < 6, so you can't take off any more 6s.

Answer = 75 remainder 2

● Decimals

The method is the same as for whole numbers, but make sure you keep the decimal points lined up.

Write 70.0 rather than 70 to help you keep everything in columns.

There is no remainder this time.

> ➤ **Example**
>
> $105.7 \div 7$
>
> $7\,\overline{)\,105.7}$
> $\underline{-\ 70.0} \qquad 10 \times 7$
> $\quad\ 35.7$
> $\underline{-\ 35.0} \qquad 5 \times 7$
> $\qquad 0.7$
> $\underline{-\ \ 0.7} \qquad 0.1 \times 7$
> $\qquad 0.0$
>
> Answer = <u>15.1</u>

---

1 Work out: **a** $112 \div 7$ **b** $207 \div 9$ **c** $118 \div 6$
2 Work out: **a** $63.5 \div 5$ **b** $120.6 \div 9$ **c** $237.6 \div 11$

TEST

Speedy Revision

Ratio & proportion

● Proportion

'What proportion?' just means
'What fraction?',
'What percentage?' or
'What decimal?'

➤ Example

1 in every 4 squares is shaded.

The proportion shaded is $\frac{1}{4}$ or 25% or 0.25.

● Ratio

In the example, 1 in every 4 squares is red.

So there is 1 red square for every 3 white squares.

The ratio of red to white squares is **1 : 3**

● Simplifying ratios

Ratios can be simplified like fractions.
Divide both sides by the same number.
If you can't divide any more you have the simplest form.

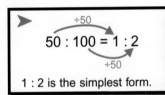

➤
÷50
50 : 100 = 1 : 2
÷50
1 : 2 is the simplest form.

● Solving problems

➤ Q & A

5 apples cost 90p.
How much would 8 apples cost?

Answer

5 apples cost:	90p
1 apple costs:	90p ÷ 5 = 18p
8 apples cost:	18p × 8 = 144p or £1.44

➤ Method

❶ Divide by 5 to find the cost of 1.
❷ Multiply by 8 to find the cost of 8.

---

1 What proportion of the squares are grey?
   Give your answer as a fraction.

2 What is the ratio of grey to white squares?
   Give your answer in its simplest form.

3 3 kg of onions cost £1.92. How much would 2 kg cost?

TEST

Calculations with brackets

● Order of operations

When faced with something like $5^2 - 2 \times (7 - 3)$ you have to work out each part in the correct order, else you'll get the wrong answer. Always do operations in this order:

Brackets $\quad\quad\quad\quad 5^2 - 2 \times (7 - 3)$
Squares $\quad\quad\quad\quad = 5^2 - 2 \times 4$
Divide and Multiply $\quad = 25 - 2 \times 4$
Add and Subtract $\quad\quad = 25 - 8$
$\quad\quad\quad\quad\quad\quad\quad = 17$

You can remember the order of operations with the word **BIDMAS**.
Brackets, then **I**ndices, **D**ivision, **M**ultiplication, **A**ddition, **S**ubtraction.
('Indices' is the fancy word for squares, cubes, etc.)

If there are several multiplications and divisions (or additions and subtractions) do them one at a time from left to right.

For example:
$24 \div 6 \div 2$
$= 4 \div 2$
$= 2$ ✔

Not:
$24 \div 6 \div 2$
$= 24 \div 3$
$= 8$ ✘

● Brackets on a calculator

Use the bracket buttons, **( )**, on your calculator exactly where they appear in a calculation. For $72 - (18 + 36)$ press:

7 2 − (1 8 + 3 6) = to get 18.

Look out for sneaky brackets:

$\frac{16 - 10}{2}$ is really $(16 - 10) \div 2$, so you have to use brackets.

Press: **(1 6 − 1 0) ÷ 2 =** ✔
Not: **1 6 − 1 0 ÷ 2 =** ✘

Work these out on paper. Check your answers on a calculator.
a $3 \times 5 - 2 \times 4$ **b** $2.8 \times (15 - 2)$ **c** $56 \div 4 \div 2$ **d** $\frac{28}{(11 + 3)}$

TEST

Checking calculations

Always check your answer. Then if you think you have made a mistake, you can find it and correct it.

● Check using inverse operations

➤ Q & A

Calculate 15.1 × 23.8.

Answer

Using a calculator:
15.1 × 23.8 = 359.38

> |◄◄ **Check**
> The inverse operation is divide:
> 359.38 ÷ 23.8 = 15.1 ✔

● Check with an equivalent calculation

➤ Q & A

Calculate 21 × 9.

Answer

21 = 20 + 1

21 × 9 = 20 × 9 + 1 × 9
      = 180 + 9
      = 189

> |◄◄ **Check**
> 9 = 10 − 1
> 21 × 9 = 21 × 10 − 21 × 1
>   = 210 − 21
>   = 189 ✔

● Check by estimating

➤ Q & A

Calculate 3189 + 4627.

Answer

Using a calculator:
3189 + 4627 = 7816

> |◄◄ **Check**
> Rounding to the nearest 1000:
> 3000 + 5000 = 8000
> 7816 is about 8000 ✔

Work these out on a calculator.
Check each answer using a suitable method.
a 49.6 + 87.2   **b** 490 × 9   **c** 924 ÷ 33

TEST

Using letters

In algebra, letters represent <u>unknown numbers</u> or numbers that can <u>change</u>.

Because the letters represent numbers, you can +, −, ×, ÷ them in exactly the same way:

$n - 1$ means <u>one less</u> than n

$n + 5$ means <u>five more</u> than n

$n + n$ means <u>two lots of n</u> or $2 \times n$

You can use 'shorthand' when <u>multiplying</u>:

For $\quad 3 \times a \quad\quad$ you write $\quad 3a \quad$ (i.e. miss out the '×').

For $\quad a \times b \times c \quad$ you write $\quad abc$

> ➤ **Example**
> Think of a number. I don't know what number you are thinking of, so I'll call it n.

● Terms and expressions

A <u>term</u> is some numbers and letters multiplied together.

$$4a + b + 3ab + 2$$

a term $\quad$ b term $\quad$ ab term $\quad$ number term

A collection of terms like this is called an <u>expression</u>.

● Collecting like terms

$4a$ and $3a$ are <u>like terms</u> because they have the <u>same letters</u>.

$2a$ and $5b$ are <u>not like terms</u> because they have <u>different letters</u>.

You can <u>simplify</u> expressions by <u>collecting like terms</u>.

$$4a \quad + \quad 3a \quad = \quad 7a$$

'<u>4</u> lots of a' and '<u>3</u> lots of a' makes '<u>7</u> lots of a'.

---

1 I have a apples. I eat one. How many are left?

2 I write n letters. Then I write 2 more. How many is that?

3 Write these in 'shorthand': **a** $p \times q$ **b** $2 \times s \times t$

4 Simplify these expressions by collecting like terms:

 a $t + t + t$ **b** $n + n + n + n$ **c** $y + 2y$ **d** $3x + 2 + x$

TEST

Solving equations

● Equations

When an <u>expression</u> is given a <u>value</u>, it is called an <u>equation</u>.

'$x + 1 = 5$' is an <u>equation</u>.

It tells you the <u>expression</u> '$x + 1$' has the <u>value</u> '5'.

● Solving equations

'<u>$x + 1$</u> = 5' means '5 is <u>one more than x</u>'.

We know that 5 is one more than 4, so x must be 4.

$x = 4$ is the <u>solution</u> to the equation $x + 1 = 5$.

Solving equations is all about finding what the value of x is.

Actually, it's not always x, it could be any letter.

➤ Q & A

Solve $7x - 4 = 10$ to find the value of x.

Answer

You need to end up with x = something.

Get rid of the − 4 by adding 4 to both sides.

$$7x - 4 = 10$$
$$7x - 4 + 4 = 10 + 4 \qquad [+4 \text{ to } \underline{\text{both}} \text{ sides}]$$
$$7x = 14$$
$$7x \div 7 = 14 \div 7 \qquad [\div \underline{\text{both}} \text{ sides by 7}]$$
$$\underline{x = 2}$$

Get rid of the × 7 by dividing both sides by 7 ($7x$ means $x \times 7$).

● Be fair with equations

You can <u>add</u>, <u>subtract</u>, <u>multiply</u> or <u>divide</u> both sides of an equation by the same number. But remember, you must do <u>exactly the same</u> thing <u>to both sides</u>.

Solve these equations.

a $2x + 5 = 11$ **b** $3x - 8 = 16$ **c** $10x = 3x + 14$

Hint: 'get rid' of the $3x$ first.

TEST

Formulae & substitution

● Formulae

A <u>formula</u> is basically a rule that <u>turns one number into another</u>.
A formula can be given <u>in words</u>, e.g. add twenty to your number,
or it can be given using <u>algebra</u> (letters), e.g. $B = A + 20$.

> ### ➤ Example
>
> Jo has a machine that makes chocolate biscuits.
> One packet of biscuit mix makes four biscuits.
>
> You can write this as a formula in words:
>
> <u>Number of biscuits = 4 × the number of packets of biscuit mix</u>
>
> You can write this with algebra by letting:
>
> <u>B</u> represents <u>the number of biscuits</u>
> <u>P</u> represents <u>the number of packets of biscuit mix</u>.
>
> Using these letters the formula is: $B = 4 \times P$ or <u>$B = 4P$</u>

● Substituting numbers into formulae & expressions

You can <u>substitute</u> a number into
an <u>expression</u> to find its value.

To substitute $y = 3$ into $y + 5$,
just write '3' in place of 'y'
then work out the answer.

> ➤ When $y = 3$: $y + 5$
> $= 3 + 5$
> $= 8$

➤ Q & A

Use the formula from the biscuit machine example above to
calculate how many chocolate biscuits you would get from
8 packets of biscuit mix.

Answer

You just put <u>8</u> in the place of <u>P</u> in the formula:
So the formula $B = 4\underline{P}$ becomes $B = 4 \times \underline{8}$
So $B = 32$, i.e. you would get <u>32 chocolate biscuits</u>.

---

1   A plumber charges £25 per hour. Write a formula, in algebra,
for the charge (C) in terms of number of hours worked (h).
2   Use your formula from **Q1** to work out the charge for 8 hours.

TEST

Speedy Revision

Sequences & number patterns (1)

A <u>sequence</u> is a list of numbers that <u>follows a pattern</u> or rule.

> Each number in a sequence is called a <u>term</u>.
>
> 2, 4, 6, 8, ...
>
> 3rd term

● Adding or subtracting patterns

This is where a number is added or subtracted to get the next term in the sequence.

1,   4,   7,   10, ...
    + 3   + 3   + 3

14,   10,   6,   2, ...
    – 4   – 4   – 4

● Multiplying or dividing patterns

Here you multiply or divide to get the next term.

2,   4,   8,   16, ...
    × 2   × 2   × 2

81,   27,   9,   3, ...
    ÷ 3   ÷ 3   ÷ 3

---

1 What is the next term in each of these sequences?
  a 5, 8, 11, 14, ... **b** 3, 6, 12, 24, ... **c** 21, 17, 13, 9, ...

2 (Read the top half of the next page before trying this question.)
  Here is a sequence of diagrams.

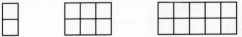

  How many squares are in the next diagram?

TEST

Sequences & number patterns (2)

● Sequence diagrams

You can also get a sequence of <u>diagrams</u>. The trick is to convert the diagrams into a sequence of <u>numbers</u>.

➤ Q & A

Here is a sequence of diagrams.

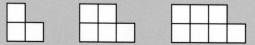

How many squares are in the next diagram in the sequence?

Answer

Count the number of squares in each diagram and write this as a sequence of numbers.

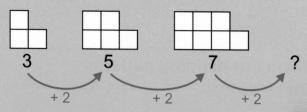

The next diagram will have 7 + 2 = <u>9 squares</u>.

Now try TEST Q2 on page 29.

Functions & mappings (1)

● Function machines

In a function machine:

◆ the <u>input</u> is the number that goes into the machine
◆ the <u>function</u> is what the machine does to the input
◆ the <u>output</u> is the result that comes out of the machine.

This function machine multiplies the input by 3:

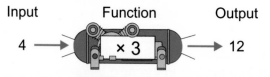

Input   Function   Output

4 ⟶   × 3   ⟶ 12

Functions & mappings (2)

● **Mapping diagrams**

A function can also be illustrated with a <u>mapping diagram</u>.
It shows the <u>outputs</u> for various <u>inputs</u>:

$$1 \longrightarrow 3$$
$$2 \longrightarrow 6$$
$$3 \longrightarrow 9$$
$$4 \longrightarrow 12$$

The function is still 'multiply by 3', as in the previous function machine.

● **Describing functions with algebra**

You can also describe functions using <u>letters</u>:

$$x \longrightarrow 3x$$

Think of this as 'x becomes 3 times x'.

▶ **Q & A**

a What is the output for this function machine when the input is 6?

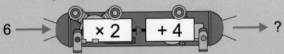

$$6 \longrightarrow \boxed{\times 2} \rightarrow \boxed{+ 4} \longrightarrow ?$$

b Write the function machine as a function using algebra.

Answer

a The machine has two steps. First '× 2', then '+ 4'.
   $6 \times 2 = 12$, $12 + 4 = \underline{16}$
b Here you need to put a letter into the machine.
   Putting x in gives $2x + 4$, so the function is $\underline{x \rightarrow 2x + 4}$.

'× 2'   '+ 4'

---

1 **a** For this function machine, what is the output when the input is 4?

$$\longrightarrow \boxed{\times 5} \rightarrow \boxed{+ 2} \longrightarrow$$

b Write the function machine as a function using algebra.

2 Draw the function in **Q1** as a mapping diagram with inputs 1, 2, 3 and 4.

TEST

Coordinates

● Coordinates

Coordinates are pairs of numbers that give the <u>positions of points</u> on a graph.

$$(x, y)$$

The <u>first number</u> of the pair is called the <u>x-coordinate</u>; the <u>second number</u> is called the <u>y-coordinate</u>. (Notice they are in alphabetical order, i.e. x comes before y.)

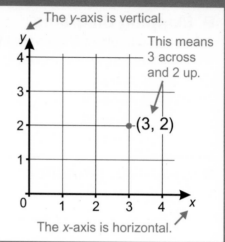

The y-axis is vertical.

This means 3 across and 2 up.

(3, 2)

The x-axis is horizontal.

● Negative coordinates

To plot points that have negative coordinates you need to extend the axes back past zero. This splits the graph into <u>4 different sections</u>.

A is at (2, 1)

B is at (−4, 1)

C is at (−2, −4)

D is at (3, −1)

Remember: the first coordinate corresponds to the horizontal axis.

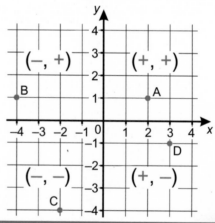

Write down the coordinates of the points on the graph on the right.

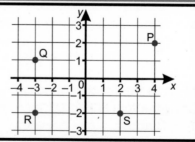

TEST

Speedy Revision

Straight-line graphs (1)

● Plotting and drawing straight-line graphs

The secret to drawing graphs is to first construct a <u>table of values</u>. This is easier than it sounds, as you are usually given a half-finished table to complete.

➤ Q & A

Complete this table of values for the equation $y = 2x + 2$ and then draw its graph.

x	–2	–1	0	1	2
$y = 2x + 2$		0		4	

Answer

The missing values are when $x = -2$, $x = 0$ and $x = 2$.
Putting these values into the equation gives:

when $x = -2$: $y = 2x + 2 = 2 \times (-2) + 2 = -4 + 2 = \underline{-2}$
when $x = 0$: $y = 2x + 2 = 2 \times 0 + 2 = 0 + 2 = \underline{2}$
when $x = 2$: $y = 2x + 2 = 2 \times 2 + 2 = 4 + 2 = \underline{6}$

So the completed table is:

x	–2	–1	0	1	2
$y = 2x + 2$	–2	0	2	4	6

Next plot the points one at a time on graph paper:

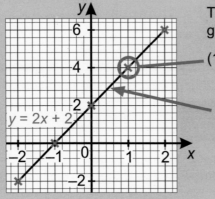

This pair of values gives the point (1, 4).

(1, 4) is plotted here.

Finally, use a <u>ruler</u> to draw a straight line through the points.

Straight-line graphs (2)

● Real-life graphs

You might be asked to draw a graph arising from a real-life situation. The most common graph you'll be faced with is a conversion graph, e.g. a graph that converts pints into litres.

The trick, again, is to first construct a <u>table of values</u>.

➤ Q & A

Christina is taking part in a sponsored run. For every mile she runs she will raise £5 for her charity.

Draw a graph to show how much money she will raise for up to 5 miles.

Answer
Construct a table of values.

She raises £5 for 1 mile so she'll raise £5 × 4 = £20 for 4 miles.

Miles run	0	1	2	3	4	5
Money raised	£0	£5	£10	£15	£20	£25

Then plot the points.

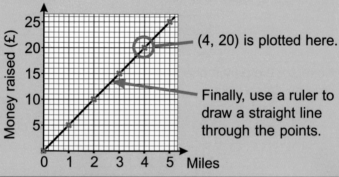

(4, 20) is plotted here.

Finally, use a ruler to draw a straight line through the points.

---

a Copy and complete the table of values for the equation $y = 3x + 2$.

x	–2	–1	0	1	2
y = 3x + 2	–4			5	

b Draw the graph of $y = 3x + 2$ on graph paper.
(The x-axis should go from –2 to 2 and the y-axis should go from –4 to 8.)

TEST

Units of measurement

● Metric units

Commonly used metric units of length are millimetre (mm), centimetre (cm), metre (m), kilometre (km); masses are gram (g), kilogram (kg); capacities are millilitre (ml), litre (l).

● Converting between metric units

Metric units are based on the decimal system and so it is easy to convert between them.

Length
10 mm = 1 cm
100 cm = 1 m
1000 m = 1 km

Mass
1000 g = 1 kg

Capacity
1000 ml = 1 litre

- To change from small units to large units divide.
- To change from large units to small units multiply.

➤ Examples

300 cm = 3 m (÷ 100)
7 litres = 7000 ml (× 1000)
5000 g = 5 kg (÷ 1000)
30 cm = 300 mm (× 10)

Divide because this is going from small to large units. The 100 comes from the fact that 100 cm = 1 m.

Multiply because this is going from large to small units. The 10 comes from the fact that 10 mm = 1 cm.

● Imperial units

Length
12 inches = 1 foot
3 feet = 1 yard

Mass
16 ounces = 1 pound

Capacity
8 pints = 1 gallon

Imperial units are getting a bit old fashioned.

● Converting between metric and imperial units

Length
1 foot is roughly 30 cm
1 mile is roughly 1.6 km

Mass
1 pound is roughly 450 g
1 ounce is roughly 30 g

Capacity
1 pint is roughly 0.5 litre
1 gallon is roughly 4.5 litres

---

1 Convert these to centimetres: **a** 2 m **b** 60 mm
2 How many grams in: **a** an ounce **b** a pound?

TEST

Appropriate units & reading scales

● Choosing the appropriate units of measurement

You need to use the correct units when measuring something.

Millimetres (mm)	Centimetres (cm)	Metres (m)	Kilometres (km)
Thickness of a book	Height of a TV	Height of a tall building	Distance to the moon

Millilitres (ml)	Litres (l)	Grams (g)	Kilograms (kg)
Liquid in a test tube	Water in a bath	Mass of a red-hot chilli	Mass of a dishwasher

● Reading scales

You should always work out how much each division is worth.

> ### Examples

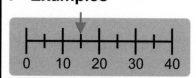

There are 2 spaces between 10 and 20.
So each space is worth 5.
The reading shows <u>15</u>.

There are 5 spaces between 20 and 30.
So each space is worth 2.
The reading shows <u>26</u>.

---

1 What unit would you use to measure the: **a** height of a giraffe **b** amount of water in a pond **c** weight of a mouse?

2 Read these scales:

a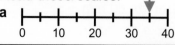

b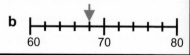

TEST

 Speedy Revision

Time & timetables

● Time facts

A common mistake in calculations is to use 100 seconds = 1 minute!

60 seconds = 1 minute
60 minutes = 1 hour
24 hours = 1 day
7 days = 1 week
52 weeks = 1 year

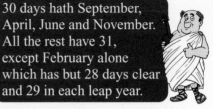

30 days hath September, April, June and November. All the rest have 31, except February alone which has but 28 days clear and 29 in each leap year.

● Two different ways of displaying the time

12-hour clocks: a.m. means in the morning
p.m. means in the afternoon or evening

24-hour clocks: In the morning, 12- and 24-hour clocks are the same.

➤ Example: 9:15 a.m. is the same as 09:15.

In the afternoon and evening, you add 12 hours to the 12-hour clock time.

The zero shows it is 24-hour time.

➤ Example: 9:15 p.m. is the same as 21:15. 9 + 12 = 21

● Timetables

This coach timetable uses 24-hour clock time.

Wigan	07:45	09:45	11:35
Bolton	08:30	10:30	12:20
Leeds	10:05	12:05	14:15

➤ Q & A

How long does the 09:45 coach from Wigan take to get to Leeds?

Answer

The coach leaves at 09:45 and arrives at 12:05.
Split this into simple stages:

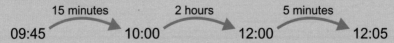

| 15 minutes | 2 hours | 5 minutes |

09:45 ➔ 10:00 ➔ 12:00 ➔ 12:05

Time = 15 minutes + 2 hours + 5 minutes = 2 hours 20 minutes

How long does the 11:35 coach take to get to Leeds?

Compass bearings & angles

● The points of a compass

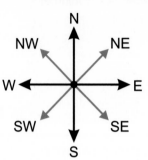

You can learn a ryhme such as Never Eat Shredded Wheat*, to remember the clockwise order of the main directions:

* This is just a ryhme, Shredded Wheat is my favourite cereal!

● Angles

An angle is a measure of turn. Angles are measured in degrees (°).

$\frac{1}{4}$ turn = 90° $\frac{1}{2}$ turn = 180° $\frac{3}{4}$ turn = 270°   Full turn = 360°

You can describe an angle by its size:

An acute angle is less than 90°.

A right angle is 90°.

An obtuse angle is between 90° and 180°.

A reflex angle is more than 180°.

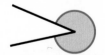

1 Which compass direction is in the opposite direction to SE?
2 How many right angles do you go through when turning from East to West?

TEST

Estimating & measuring angles

● Estimating angles

➤ Q & A

Estimate the size of these angles:

a **b**

Answer

You need to compare the angles to 90°, 180°, 270° and 360°.

a The angle is less than 90°; it looks about $\frac{2}{3}$ the size of 90° so a good estimate would be <u>60°</u>.

b The angle is more than 180° but less than 270°. A good estimate would be <u>210°</u>.

● Measuring angles with a protractor

Before measuring you must <u>estimate</u> the size of the angle.

This angle is acute. It looks about 45° (half a right angle).

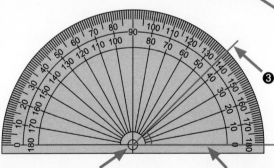

❸ Read the angle from the correct scale. The estimate was 45° so it must be <u>44°</u> (not 136°).

❶ The point of the angle should be at the cross.

❷ One arm of the angle should be along the 0° line.

---

1 Estimate the size of these angles.

a **b**

2 Measure the angles in **Q1** with a protractor.

TEST

Calculating angles

❶ Angles on a straight line add up to 180°

In the diagram: 138° + 42° = 180°

❷ Angles in a triangle add up to 180°

In the diagram: 40° + 45° + 95° = 180°
(Try the activity on page 61.)

❸ Angles around a point add up to 360°

In the diagram: 90° + 140° + 130° = 360°

❹ Vertically opposite angles are equal

Vertically opposite angles are formed
when two straight lines cross.

In the diagram: 40° = 40° and 140° = 140°

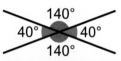

➤ Q & A

Calculate the size of the missing angles:

a   b   c

Answer

a The angles in a triangle add up to 180°, so 45° + 65° + ? = 180°.
   So the missing angle is 180°− 45° − 65° = <u>70°</u>.
b Angles on a straight line add up to 180°, so 46° + ? = 180°.
   So the missing angle is 180° − 46° = <u>134°</u>.
c Angles around a point add up to 360°, so 87° + 135° + ? = 360°.
   So the missing angle is 360° − 87° − 135° = <u>138°</u>.

Work out the missing angles.

a    b   c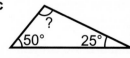

TEST

40

Symmetry

● Reflection symmetry

If a shape can be folded so that one half fits exactly on the other, it is said to have <u>reflection symmetry</u> (also known as <u>line symmetry</u>).

Fold line (also called mirror line)

Some shapes have more than one line of symmetry; some don't have any:

Square
4 lines of symmetry

Equilateral triangle
3 lines of symmetry

No lines of symmetry

● Rotation symmetry

A shape has rotation symmetry if it looks exactly the same when turned. The <u>order of rotation symmetry</u> is the number of times a shape fits exactly over itself during a full-turn about its centre.

▶ Q & A

What is the order of rotation symmetry of these shapes?

Order 4

Order 3

Order 1

Note: Order of rotation symmetry 1 means <u>no rotation symmetry</u>.

● Tracing paper makes it easy

Reflection symmetry: trace half of the shape on tracing paper, then turn the paper over to see if it fits exactly on to the other half.

Rotation symmetry: trace the shape, then rotate the tracing paper.

For each shape write down the: **i** number of lines of symmetry **ii** order of rotation symmetry.

a

b

c

TEST

Triangles & other polygons

● Four types of triangle

Right-angled
One 90° angle

Equilateral
3 equal sides
3 equal angles

Isosceles
2 equal sides
2 equal angles

Scalene
All sides and angles
are different.

● Quadrilaterals (shapes with 4 sides)

Square
4 lines of symmetry
Rotation symmetry
of order 4
All angles are 90°
All sides equal
2 pairs of parallel sides

Rhombus
2 lines of symmetry
Rotation symmetry
of order 2
All sides equal
Opposite angles equal
2 pairs of parallel sides

Rectangle
2 lines of symmetry
Rotation symmetry
of order 2
All angles are 90°
Opposite sides equal
2 pairs of parallel sides

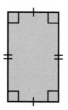

Kite
1 line of symmetry
No rotation symmetry
2 pairs of adjacent sides
equal
1 pair of opposite angles equal

Trapezium
No lines of symmetry
(unless isosceles)
No rotation symmetry
One pair of parallel sides

Parallelogram
No lines of symmetry
Rotation symmetry
of order 2
Opposite sides
equal and parallel
Opposite angles equal

Parallel lines never meet.
Perpendicular lines cross at right angles.

● Regular polygons

All sides and all angles in a regular
polygon are the same. Two examples
are the square and equilateral triangle.

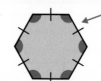

A regular
hexagon has
six equal sides
and angles.

Reflection

● Reflecting a shape in a mirror line

When you reflect a shape in a mirror line its size and shape are <u>not</u> changed. The original shape is called the <u>object</u> and its reflection is called the <u>image</u>.

➤ Q & A

Reflect the shape in the mirror line.

Answer

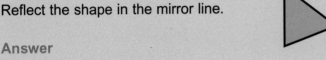

❶ Draw a line from each corner <u>at right angles</u> to the mirror line.
❷ Extend the lines exactly the same distance on the other side of the mirror line.
❸ Join up the ends of the lines to show the image.

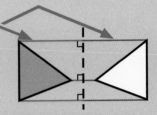

● Two mirror lines

You can make a symmetrical pattern by reflecting in two mirror lines.

Keep reflecting until the pattern is complete.

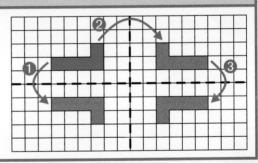

Copy and then reflect these shapes in the mirror lines:

a   **b**

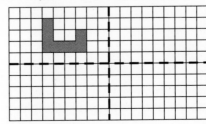

TEST

Rotation

● Turning shapes

A rotation turns a shape through an angle about some fixed point.
A rotation can be in a <u>clockwise</u> or <u>anticlockwise</u> direction.

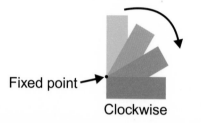

Fixed point →

Clockwise   Anticlockwise

➤ Q & A

Rotate the shape 90° <u>clockwise</u>
about the corner marked with a dot.

Answer

❶ Draw around the shape on
  tracing paper.
❷ Pin the tracing paper down with
  your pencil at the dot.
❸ Rotate the tracing paper 90°
  clockwise.
❹ Draw over the traced shape
  (press down quite hard) so that
  you can see where to draw the
  rotated shape.

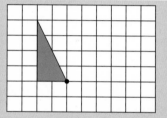

90° clockwise

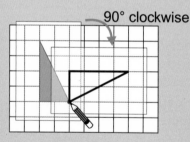

Rotate these shapes 90° <u>anticlockwise</u> about the dots:

a
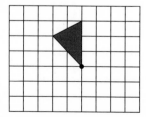

b
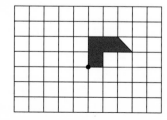

TEST

44

Speedy Revision

Translation

● Sliding shapes

A translation is where you slide a shape along <u>without</u> rotating or reflecting it.

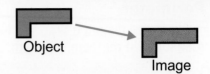

Object

Image

A translation moves a shape:
1. a specific distance <u>left or right</u>
2. and then a specific distance <u>up or down</u>.

➤ Q & A

Translate the triangle 5 squares to the right and 3 squares up.

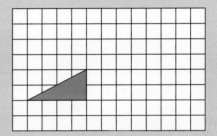

Answer

1. Put your pencil on a corner of the shape.
2. Move your pencil 5 squares right and 3 squares up.
3. Draw the shape in the new position.

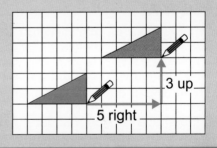

3 up

5 right

---

1 Translate the shape 4 units to the right and 2 units up.

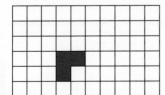

2 Translate the shape 5 units to the left and 2 units down.

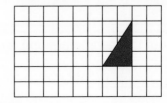

TEST

Perimeter & area

● Perimeter

Perimeter is the distance around the outside edge of a 2-D shape. It is measured in mm, cm, m or km.

➤ Q & A

What is the perimeter of this shape?

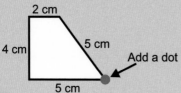

Answer

Start at the dot and add the sides up clockwise: 5 + 4 + 2 + 5 = 16 cm

➤ Method

❶ Mark a corner with a dot.

❷ Start at the dot, add the sides as you go around the shape. Stop when you get back to the dot.

❸ Essential: Show your working.

● Area

The area of a 2-D shape is the amount of space it covers. It is measured in mm², cm², m² or km². ◄── Notice the 'squared' bit.

➤ Q & A

What is the area of this rectangle?

Answer

One method is to count the number of squares. There are 18 of them, so the area is 18 cm².

If the shape isn't on a square grid, you'll need to use this formula:

> **Area of a rectangle = length × width**

For example, the area of this rectangle = 5 × 2 = 10 cm².

2 cm
5 cm

Work out the perimeters and areas of these shapes.

a 4 cm 10 cm

b 2 cm 2 cm 4 cm 10 cm

TEST

46

3-D shapes & nets

● Nets

A <u>net</u> is a 3-D shape folded out <u>flat</u>.
(It helps to imagine that the shape is
made out of cardboard.)

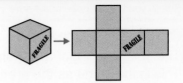

Below are some 3-D shapes, with their nets, that you need to know.

Cube

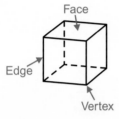

There are 11 different nets for a cube.
Here are two, can you draw the others? (See p61)

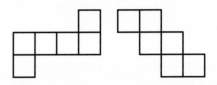

Cuboid

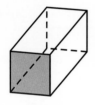

Square-based pyramid

Triangular prism

 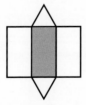

Regular tetrahedron

How many faces, edges and vertices do these have?

a cuboid **b** triangular prism

TEST

Surface area

Before you try this page make sure you understand everything on the previous page.

● **Surface area**

The <u>surface area</u> of a 3-D shape is the <u>total area</u> of all its <u>faces</u>. This is the same as the <u>area of its net</u>.

➤ **Q & A**

Work out the surface area of this cuboid.

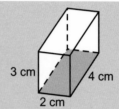

Answer

First sketch the net of the cuboid.

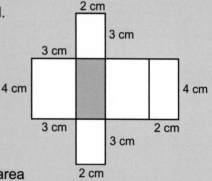

The task now is to work out the area of each of the six rectangles (faces).

Two have an area of 2 cm × 3 cm = 6 cm²
two have an area of 2 cm × 4 cm = 8 cm²
and two have an area of 3 cm × 4 cm = 12 cm².

So the total surface area is 6 + 6 + 8 + 8 + 12 + 12 = <u>52 cm²</u>.

Work out the surface area of each of these shapes:

a

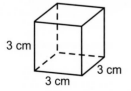

b

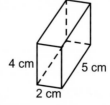

TEST

Frequency tables

● Frequency tables

Frequency tables display data that has been counted.

➤ Tallies

Always use tallies when you are counting items of data. You should group your tallies in fives.

➤ Q & A

Here are the favourite colours of 20 people.

red, red, blue, green, blue, green, blue, blue, red, green, red, red, blue, green, blue, red, green, blue, red, red

Show the data in a frequency table.

Answer

Use a tally column to help you count.

Colour	Tally	Frequency
Red	ⵂ‖‖	8
Blue	ⵂ‖	7
Green	ⵂ	5
	Total	20

Write the tallies as numbers in the frequency column.

Total the numbers in the frequency column.
This helps make sure you haven't made a mistake.
The question said 20 people so this is correct.

● Grouping data

If you are given a long list of numbers, you can group the numbers into intervals such as $20 \leqslant n < 30$.

For example, this list:

22, 14, 15, 23, 33, 14, 37, 36, 22, 25, 31, 6, 13, 8, 23, 23, 30, 20

is shown in the frequency table.

Number, n	Tally	Frequency
$0 \leqslant n < 10$	‖	2
$10 \leqslant n < 20$	‖‖	4
$20 \leqslant n < 30$	ⵂ‖	7
$30 \leqslant n < 40$	ⵂ	5
	Total	18

Note: 20 belongs to $20 \leqslant n < 30$, not $10 \leqslant n < 20$.

Show this data in a frequency table (group as in the example above): 20, 12, 3, 45, 32, 9, 12, 5, 23, 25, 32, 31, 40, 32, 12, 33

TEST

Pictograms & bar charts

Once you've got your data into a frequency table (see previous page) you can set about turning it into a nice chart or diagram.

● Pictograms

In a pictogram the frequencies are represented by <u>pictures</u>, where each picture represents a certain number of items.

Number of dogs owned per street

Rover Lane
Poodle Close
Mongrel Way

Key:
🐕 = 2 dogs

This means there are 7 dogs in Mongrel Way

● Bar charts

In a bar chart the <u>frequencies</u> from your frequency table are represented by the <u>heights of the bars</u>.

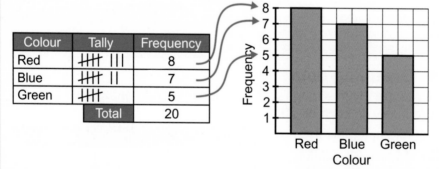

Colour	Tally	Frequency
Red	ⅣⅠ |||	8
Blue	ⅣⅠ ||	7
Green	ⅣⅠ	5
Total		20

Bar line graphs are similar to bar charts except lines are drawn instead of bars.

The frequency table shows the number of medals that Hungary won at the 2004 Athens Olympics. Draw a pictogram (with one symbol representing 2 medals) and a bar chart to display the data.

Medal	Frequency
Gold	8
Silver	6
Bronze	3

TEST

Speedy Revision

Pie charts & line graphs

● Interpreting pie charts

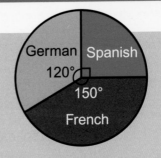

➤ Q & A

The pie chart shows the favourite language of 24 students.

How many students prefer
a Spanish **b** German?

Answer

a Spanish is a quarter of the pie chart, so a quarter of the students prefer Spanish, i.e. $\frac{1}{4}$ of 24 = <u>6 students</u> prefer Spanish.

b German takes up 120° of the pie chart. This is $\frac{120°}{360°} = \frac{1}{3}$ as a fraction of the pie chart, so $\frac{1}{3}$ of 24 = <u>8 students</u> prefer German.

> 360° is the whole of the circle.
>
> Fraction = $\dfrac{\text{Angle}}{360°}$

● Line graphs

A line graph is a set of <u>points joined with straight lines</u>.

This type of graph is very good for showing <u>trends</u> over periods of <u>time</u>.

The line graph on the right shows that the number of late students falls as the week goes along.

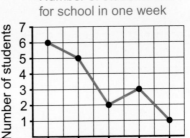

Number of students late for school in one week

The pie chart shows the type of bicycles owned by 36 students.

How many students own:
a BMX bikes
b mountain bikes?

(You should assume that students own only one type of bike.)

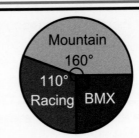

TEST

Mean, median, mode, range (1)

Mean = $\dfrac{\textbf{total of the values}}{\textbf{number of values}}$

You need to learn these.

Median = the middle value when the numbers are put in order of size

Mode = the most common value

Range = highest value – lowest value

When people talk about 'the average' they're usually referring to 'the mean'. But be careful, because the median and mode are also 'averages'.

► Q & A

Find the mean, median, mode and range of this set of data:

5, 2, 3, 1, 5, 5, 10, 2, 3

Answer

Mean

The total of the values = 5 + 2 + 3 + 1 + 5 + 5 + 10 + 2 + 3 = 36
The number of values = 9 (count the numbers in the list)
So the mean = 36 ÷ 9 = 4.

Median

Rearrange the numbers in order of size.
1, 2, 2, 3, 3, 5, 5, 5,10
The middle number is 3, so the median = 3.

| If there are an even number of values, the median is halfway between the middle two. e.g. the median of 2, 3, 4, 5 is (3 + 4) ÷ 2 = 3.5. |

Mode

The most common value is 5 (there are three of them). So the mode = 5.

Range

The highest value = 10 and the lowest value = 1.
So the range = 10 – 1 = 9.

Find the mode, median, mean and range of this set of data:
5, 6, 7, 4, 4, 12, 4

TEST

Mean, median, mode, range (2)

● Using the appropriate average

- ● The <u>mean</u> is useful as it takes all the values into account, but it can be distorted by extreme values, e.g. you wouldn't use the mean for this data: 1, 2, 2, 3, 5, 909.
- ● The <u>median</u> is useful when there are extreme values (as in the above example).
- ● The <u>mode</u> is useful when you just want the most common value, e.g. the week's best selling DVD.

● Finding the mean from a frequency table

The frequency table below shows the number of televisions per household in Lance's street.

Number of TVs	0	1	2	3
Frequency (number of households)	2	7	4	2

This means that 7 households have 1 TV.

The total number of TVs = (0 × 2) + (1 × 7) + (2 × 4) + (3 × 2) = 21
The total number of households = 2 + 7 + 4 + 2 = 15
So the mean number of TVs per household is 21 ÷ 15 = 1.4 TVs.

Find the mean number of TVs per household in Sarah's street:

Number of TVs	0	1	2	3
Frequency (number of households)	1	6	5	4

TEST

Probability (1)

<u>Probability</u> is to do with the chance of something happening.

You can use words to describe different probabilities, such as: *impossible, very unlikely, unlikely, evens, likely, very likely, certain.*

Probabilities can also be given as <u>fractions or decimals</u>, but they are always <u>between 0 and 1</u>. If something has <u>probability 0</u> it <u>can't happen</u>; if it has <u>probability 1</u> it will <u>definitely happen</u>.

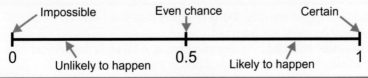

Impossible   Even chance   Certain

0   0.5   1
    Unlikely to happen   Likely to happen

Probability (2)

● Calculating probabilities

Probability of an event = $\dfrac{\text{Number of ways an event can happen}}{\text{Total number of possible outcomes}}$

➤ Q & A

You throw a fair dice. What is the probability of getting:
a a 6 **b** an even number?

Answer

When throwing a dice there are 6 possible outcomes: 1, 2, 3, 4, 5, 6

a There is only one way of getting a 6.   P(6) is a short way of writing
  P(6) = $\frac{1}{6}$ 'the probability of getting 6'.

b There are 3 ways of getting an even number: 2, 4 or 6.
  P(even) = $\frac{3}{6}$ = $\frac{1}{2}$ Use the formula!

● Experimental probability

You can estimate probabilities from experimental data.
For example, the table shows the results when a spinner was spun
100 times:

Colour	Red	Black	Grey
Frequency	35	60	5

From the table, you can estimate that the probability that the
spinner lands on black is $\frac{60}{100}$ = $\frac{3}{5}$.

> Theoretical and experimental probabilities should be similar,
> but are unlikely to be the same.

For example, if you toss a coin 100 times and get heads 48 times,
you shouldn't think that the coin is unfair (biased).
Increasing the number of times an experiment is repeated generally
leads to better estimates of probability.

---

1 Use a word(s) to descibe the probability that the next baby born at
  your local hospital will be a girl.
2 A bag contains 2 red and 4 green beads. A bead is drawn from the
  bag at random. What is the probability that the bead is red?

TEST

Speedy revision test (1)

These questions test the basic facts. The simple truth is that the more of them you can answer, the better you'll do in your SATs. So try them as often as you can. (The answers can be found on the pages given at the end of each question.)

1 Write 32 549 in words. (p4)
2 Write 31.62 in words. (p4)
3 How far, and which way, should the digits move when dividing by 1000? (p5)
4 What is 14.2 ÷ 10? (p5)
5 Use partitioning to work out 683 − 274. (p6)
6 Use compensation to work out 718 − 496. (p6)
7 When using a written method to + or −, what do you need to line up first? (p7)
8 Use a written method to work out 4.72 + 3.51. (p7)
9 What does the symbol $\leqslant$ mean? (p8)
10 Which is greater, 4.16 or 4.128? (p8)
11 4315 is exactly halfway between 4310 and 4320.
   What is 4315 rounded to the nearest 10? (p9)
12 Round 6790 to the nearest 1000. (p9)
13 Round 6.2 to the nearest whole number. (p10)
14 Round 3.27 to one decimal place. (p10)
15 Which of these is correct: −10 < −5 or −10 > −5? (p11)
16 Work out −3 + 5. (p11)
17 Work out −1 − 7. (p11)
18 What do even numbers end in? (p12)
19 What do odd numbers end in? (p12)
20 What are the first five square numbers? (p12)
21 What are the first five triangular numbers? (p12)
22 What are the first five prime numbers? (p12)
23 Fill in the blank in this sentence:
   The _____ of a number are the numbers in its times-table. (p13)
24 What are the first three multiples of 3? (p13)
25 Fill in the blank in this sentence:
   The _____ of a number are the numbers that divide into it exactly
   (including 1 and itself). (p13)
26 Write down all the factors of 10. (p13)
27 Work out 30^2. (p14)
28 What is the square root of 16? (p14)
29 Work out the square root of 169 on your calculator. (p14)
30 The denominator is the top of the fraction. True or false? (p15)
31 Write $\frac{15}{45}$ in its simplest form. (p15)
32 Complete this sentence: You can only add or subtract fractions if they have
   the same _____. (p16)
33 Work out $\frac{5}{8} - \frac{3}{8}$. (p16)
34 Name the sort of fraction that's described here:
   The numerator is bigger than the denominator. (p17)

Speedy revision test (2)

35 Write $\frac{5}{2}$ as a mixed number. (p17)

36 Which is smaller, $\frac{3}{8}$ or $\frac{1}{2}$? (p17)

37 What does 'per cent' mean? (p18)

38 What is two-thirds of £60? (p18)

39 To find 10% of something, what do you divide by? (p18)

40 To find 25% of something, what do you divide by? (p18)

41 What is 75% as a fraction? (p19)

42 Write 0.12 as a fraction. (p19)

43 What is the quick way to multiply something by 11? (p20)

44 Use a written method to work out 29 × 42. (p21)

45 Use a written method to work out 452 ÷ 6 (there will be a remainder). (p22)

46 What is the ratio of grey to white squares in this diagram? (p23)

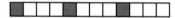

47 Five apples cost 90p. How much would eight apples cost? (p23)

48 What does BIDMAS stand for? (p24)

49 Work out $5^2 - 2 \times (7 - 3)$ using BIDMAS. (p24)

50 Which of these is correct? 'Always check your answer' or 'The moon is made of cheese'. (p25)

51 In algebra, what is a 'term'? (p26)

52 In algebra, what is an 'expression'? (p26)

53 Solve $7x - 4 = 10$. (p27)

54 Given that $B = 4P$, work out the value of B when $P = 8$. (p28)

55 What is the next term in each of these sequences?

   a 1, 4, 7, ...   **b** 14, 10, 6, ...   **c** 2, 4, 8, ...   **d** 81, 27, 9, ...   (p29)

56 Here is a sequence of diagrams:

   How many squares are in the next diagram in the sequence? (p30)

57 a   What is the output for this function machine when the input is 6? (p31)

   b   Write the function machine as a function using algebra. (p31)

58 Mark these points on a copy of the graph:
   A(2, 1), B(−4, 1), C(−2, −4)
   and D(3, −1). (p32)

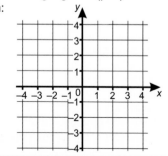

Speedy revision test (3)

59 What should you construct before drawing a graph? (p33)
60 State the missing units: 10 mm = 1 ___, 100 cm = 1 ___, 1000 m = 1 ___ (p35)
61 What sort of units are those given in the previous question? (p35)
62 How many grams in a kilogram? (p35)
63 How many inches in a foot? (p35)
64 Roughly how many litres are there in a pint? (p35)
65 What is the reading on the scale on the right? (p36)
66 How many weeks in a year? (p37)
67 How many days in July? (p37)
68 What does a.m. mean? (p37)
69 Write 9:15 p.m. as a 24-hour clock time. (p37)
70 Label the points of this compass: (p38)

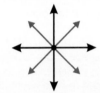

71 Draw diagrams to show acute, right, obtuse and reflex angles. (p38)
72 Before measuring an angle with a protractor, what must you do? (p39)
73 What do the angles on a straight line add up to? (p40)
74 What do the angles in a triangle add up to? (p40)
75 What do the angles around a point add up to? (p40)
76 Draw a diagram to show vertically opposite angles. (p40)
77 If a shape can be folded so that one half fits exactly on the other, what is it said to have? (p41)
78 What is the order of rotation symmetry of each of these shapes? (p41)

79 How many equal sides does an isosceles triangle have? (p42)
80 How many equal sides does a rhombus have? (p42)
81 What sort of lines never meet? (p42)
82 What's the same in a regular polygon? (p42)
83 Make a symmetrical pattern
by reflecting the shape in
both mirror lines. (p43)

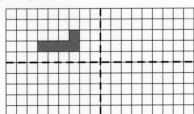

Speedy revision test (4)

84 Rotate the shape 90° clockwise about the corner marked with a dot. (p44)

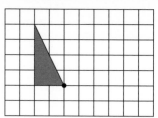

85 Fill in the blanks. A translation moves a shape:
   ❶ a specific distance _____ or _____
   ❷ and then a specific distance _____ or _____. (p45)

86 What should you do first when working out the perimeter of a shape? (p46)

87 What is the formula for the area of a rectangle? (p46)

88 Sketch nets of a cuboid and a regular tetrahedron. (p47)

89 Complete: The surface area of a 3-D shape is the total area of all its faces. This is the same as the area of its _____. (p48)

90 What comes in fives and should be used to help count items of data? (p49)

91 Which group does 20 belong to: $10 \leqslant n < 20$ or $20 \leqslant n < 30$? (p49)

92 By what are the frequencies represented in a pictogram? (p50)

93 What do the heights of the bars represent in a bar chart? (p50)

94 The pie chart shows the favourite language of 24 students.
   How many students prefer Spanish?

95 What is a line graph good at showing? (p51)

96 How do you work out the mean, median, mode and range? (p52)

97 The probability of something happening is 0. What does this mean? (p53)

98 What is the formula for calculating the probability of an event happening? (p54)

99 You throw a fair dice. What is the probability of getting a 6? (p54)

TEST answers

Page 5 Place value (2)
1 a Ninety-two
  b One thousand, six hundred and three
  c Fifteen point six seven
2 a 410 b 2.8
3 a 390 b 8000 c 71 d 150
  e 42 f 64 g 1.63 h 1.49

Page 6 Mental strategies for + and –
1 a 485 b 487 c 847 d 364
2 a 131 b 553 c 425 d 265

Page 7 Written methods for + and –
1 a 394 b 877 c 438 d 611
2 a 7.89 b 3.84 c 0.25 d 12.27

Page 8 Ordering numbers
1 34 300
2 33, 209, 516, 888, 1460
3 23.25

Page 9 Rounding & estimating (1)
1 a 80 b 440 c 1070
2 a 1000 b 1000 c 17 000
3 489 + 204 is roughly 500 + 200 which is 700, so 936 must be incorrect.

Page 10 Rounding & estimating (2)
1 a 3 b 8 c 3 d 18 e 27 f 3 g 5
2 a 4.6 b 6.5 c 1.3 d 4.0

Page 11 Negative numbers
1 –10
2 –5, –4, 0, 2, 3
3 a –8 + 3 = –5

$-9 \ -8 \ -7 \ -6 \ -5 \ -4$

  b –2 – 3 = –5

$-6 \ -5 \ -4 \ -3 \ -2 \ -1$

Page 12 Special numbers
1 a 2, 4, 6, 8, 10, 12, 14, 16, 18, 20
  b 1, 3, 5, 7, 9, 11, 13, 15, 17, 19
  c 1, 4, 9, 16, 25, 36, 49, 64, 81, 100
  d 1, 3, 6, 10, 15, 21, 28, 36, 45, 55
2 a 32, 36, 64 b 49, 17, 21, 3 c 49, 36, 64
  d 21, 36, 3 e 17, 3

Page 13 Multiples & factors
1 a 5, 10, 15, 20, 25 b 8, 16, 24, 32, 40
  c 6, 12, 18, 24, 30 d 9, 18, 27, 36, 45
2 2, 3, 5 & 10 are factors of 270, but 4 is not.
3 a 1, 2, 4, 8 b 1, 2, 4, 8, 16, 32
  c 1, 2, 4, 5, 8, 10, 20, 40

Page 14 Squares & square roots
1 a 25 b 121 c 64 d 1600
2 a 6 b 7 c 12

Page 15 Fractions (1)
1 $\frac{5}{8}$ 2 a $\frac{2}{3}$ b $\frac{3}{4}$ c $\frac{2}{5}$

Page 16 Fractions (2)
1 a $\frac{2}{7}$ b $\frac{3}{5}$ c $\frac{5}{9}$
2 a $\frac{5}{9}$ b $\frac{2}{5}$ c $\frac{7}{8}$
3 $\frac{2}{5}$

Page 17 Fractions (3)
1 $\frac{5}{3}$ 2 $3\frac{1}{3}$ 3 $\frac{1}{2}, \frac{3}{4}, \frac{7}{8}$

Page 18 Fractions, decimals & percentages (1)
1 a 24 cm b 72 cm 2 £4 3 £42

Page 19 Fractions, decimals & percentages (2)
1 a $\frac{11}{100}$ b $\frac{5}{100} = \frac{1}{20}$ c $\frac{6}{10} = \frac{3}{5}$ d $\frac{15}{100} = \frac{3}{20}$
2 a 0.7 b 70%
3 $\frac{35}{100} = \frac{7}{20}$

Page 20 Mental strategies for × and ÷
1 a 56 b 207 c 770 d 204
2 a 7 b 8 c 11

Page 21 Written multiplication
1 a 828 b 1694 c 44.94

Page 22 Written division
1 a 16 b 23 c 19 remainder 4
2 a 12.7 b 13.4 c 21.6

Page 23 Ratio & proportion
1 $\frac{2}{3}$
2 2 : 1
3 £1.28

Page 24 Calculations with brackets
a 7 b 36.4 c 7 d 2

Page 25 Checking calculations
a 136.8 b 4410 c 28

Page 26 Using letters
1 $a - 1$ 2 $n + 2$ 3 a pq b $2st$
4 a $3t$ b $4n$ c $3y$ d $4x + 2$

Page 27 Solving equations
a $x = 3$ b $x = 8$ c $x = 2$

Page 28 Formulae & substitution
1 $C = 25h$ 2 £200

Page 29 Sequences & number patterns (1)
1 a 17 b 48 c 5
2 14

TEST answers

Page 31 Functions & mappings (2)
1   **a** 22   **b** $x \to 5x + 2$
2   $1 \to 7$
    $2 \to 12$
    $3 \to 17$
    $4 \to 22$

Page 32 Coordinates
P(4, 2), Q(−3, 1), R(−3, −2), S(2, −2)

Page 34 Straight-line graphs (2)
a

x	−2	−1	0	1	2
$y = 3x + 2$	−4	−1	2	5	8

b

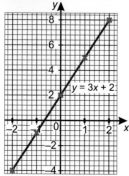

Page 35 Units of measurement
1   **a** 200 cm   **b** 6 cm
2   **a** Roughly 30 g   **b** Roughly 450 g

Page 36 Appropriate units & reading scales
1   **a** metres   **b** litres   **c** grams
2   **a** 35   **b** 68

Page 37 Time & timetables
2 hours 40 minutes

Page 38 Compass bearings & angles
1   NW (North-West)
2   2 right angles

Page 39 Estimating & measuring angles
1   **a** Between 70° & 80°
    b Between 160° & 170°
2   **a** 75°   **b** 165°

Page 40 Calculating angles
a 60°   **b** 135°   **c** 105°

Page 41 Symmetry
a **i** 2 **ii** 2   **b** **i** 1 **ii** 1   **c** **i** 3 **ii** 3

Page 43 Reflection
a

b

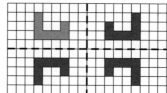

Page 44 Rotation
a

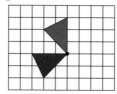

b

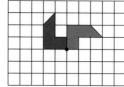

Page 45 Translation
1

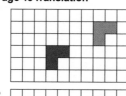

2

Page 46 Perimeter & area
a   Perimeter = 28 cm, area = 40 cm²
b   Perimeter = 28 cm, area = 24 cm²

Speedy Revision

TEST answers

Page 47 3-D shapes & nets
a 6 faces, 12 edges, 8 vertices
b 5 faces, 9 edges, 6 vertices

The 11 nets of a cube are:

Page 48 Surface area
a 54 cm²
b 76 cm²

Page 49 Frequency tables

Number, n	Tally	Frequency
0 ≤ n < 10	III	3
10 ≤ n < 20	III	3
20 ≤ n < 30	III	3
30 ≤ n < 40	HHT	5
40 ≤ n < 50	II	2
	Total	16

Page 50 Pictograms & bar charts

Medals for Hungary at 2004 Olympics

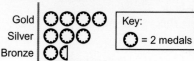

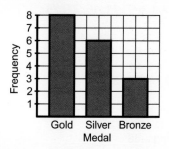

Page 51 Pie charts & line graphs
a 9
b 16

Page 52 Mean, median, mode, range (1)
Mode = 4, median = 5, mean = 6, range = 8

Page 53 Mean, median, mode, range (2)
1.75 TVs

Page 54 Probability (2)
1 Evens, even chance or fifty-fifty
2 $\frac{2}{6} = \frac{1}{3}$

---

❶ Draw a large triangle on a piece of paper (use a ruler!).

❷ Carefully cut out the triangle.

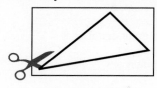

❸ Tear off the 3 corners of the triangle.

❹ Place the cut off corners together so that they form a straight line.

Straight line

❺ As there are 180° on a straight line, you have shown that <u>the angles in a triangle add up to 180°</u>.

ACTIVITY

Index

Speedy Revision

Index

Index

Index